THE FSB

Felix Dzerzhinsky, head of Russia's first spy agency

THE FSB

ODYSSEYS

KRISSY EBERTH

CREATIVE EDUCATION · CREATIVE PAPERBACKS

Published by Creative Education and Creative Paperbacks
P.O. Box 227, Mankato, Minnesota 56002
Creative Education and Creative Paperbacks
are imprints of The Creative Company
www.thecreativecompany.us

Design by Graham Morgan
Art direction by Tom Morgan
Edited by Jill Kalz

Images by Alamy Stock Photo/Mihail Chekalov, 6; Dreamstime/Stuart Monk,
27; Getty Images/Ben Martin, cover, 42, Bettmann, 24-25, FBI, 55, Global
Images Ukraine, 75, Hulton Deutsch, 62, Keystone, 11, 61, Laski Diffusion, 2,
Michael Stephens - PA Images, 52, Natasja Weitsz, 70-71, Sasha Mordovets,
72; Unsplash/ROBIN WORRALL, 44; Wikimedia Commons/Alexander
Litovchenko, 8-9, Leo Medvedev/Лев Леонидович Медведев, 22, National
Nuclear Security Administration/Nevada Site Office, 58-59, NSSDC, NASA, 35,
PatrickCaproni, 66, public domain/Marina Oswald, 49, Razumhak, 4-5,
SpetsnazAlpha, 30-31, unknown author, 12-13, 17, 46, Фотография ателье
Буллы, 18

Every effort has been made to contact copyright holders for material
reproduced in this book. Any omissions will be rectified in subsequent
printings if notice is given to the publisher.

Library of Congress Cataloging-in-Publication Data
Names: Eberth, Krissy, author.
Title: The FSB / Krissy Eberth.
Description: Mankato, Minnesota : Creative Education and Creative
    Paperbacks, [2025] | Series: Odysseys in Spycraft | Includes
    bibliographical references and index. | Audience: Ages 12-15 |
    Audience: Grades 7-9 | Summary: "Unlock the spy secrets of Russia's
    Federal Security Service (FSB), from the espionage agency's history of
    intelligence gathering to counterterrorism training and key missions.
    Includes a glossary, sidebars, index, and further resources"—Provided
    by publisher.
Identifiers: LCCN 2024018500 (print) | LCCN 2024018501 (ebook) | ISBN
    9798889892908 (library binding) | ISBN 9781682776568 (paperback) |
    ISBN 9798889894018 (ebook)
Subjects: LCSH: Federal'naĭá sluzhba bezopasnosti Rossii—Juvenile
    literature. | Intelligence service—Russia (Federation)—Juvenile
    literature. | Secret service—Russia (Federation)—Juvenile literature.
Classification: LCC JN6695.A55 E24 2025 (print) | LCC JN6695.A55
    (ebook) | DDC 327.1247—dc23/eng/20240508
LC record available at https://lccn.loc.gov/2024018500
LC ebook record available at https://lccn.loc.gov/2024018501

Printed in the United States of America

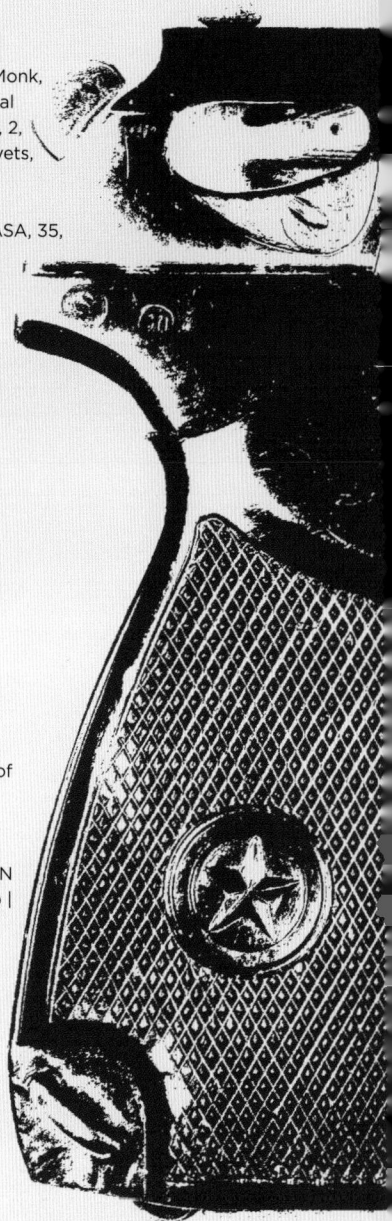

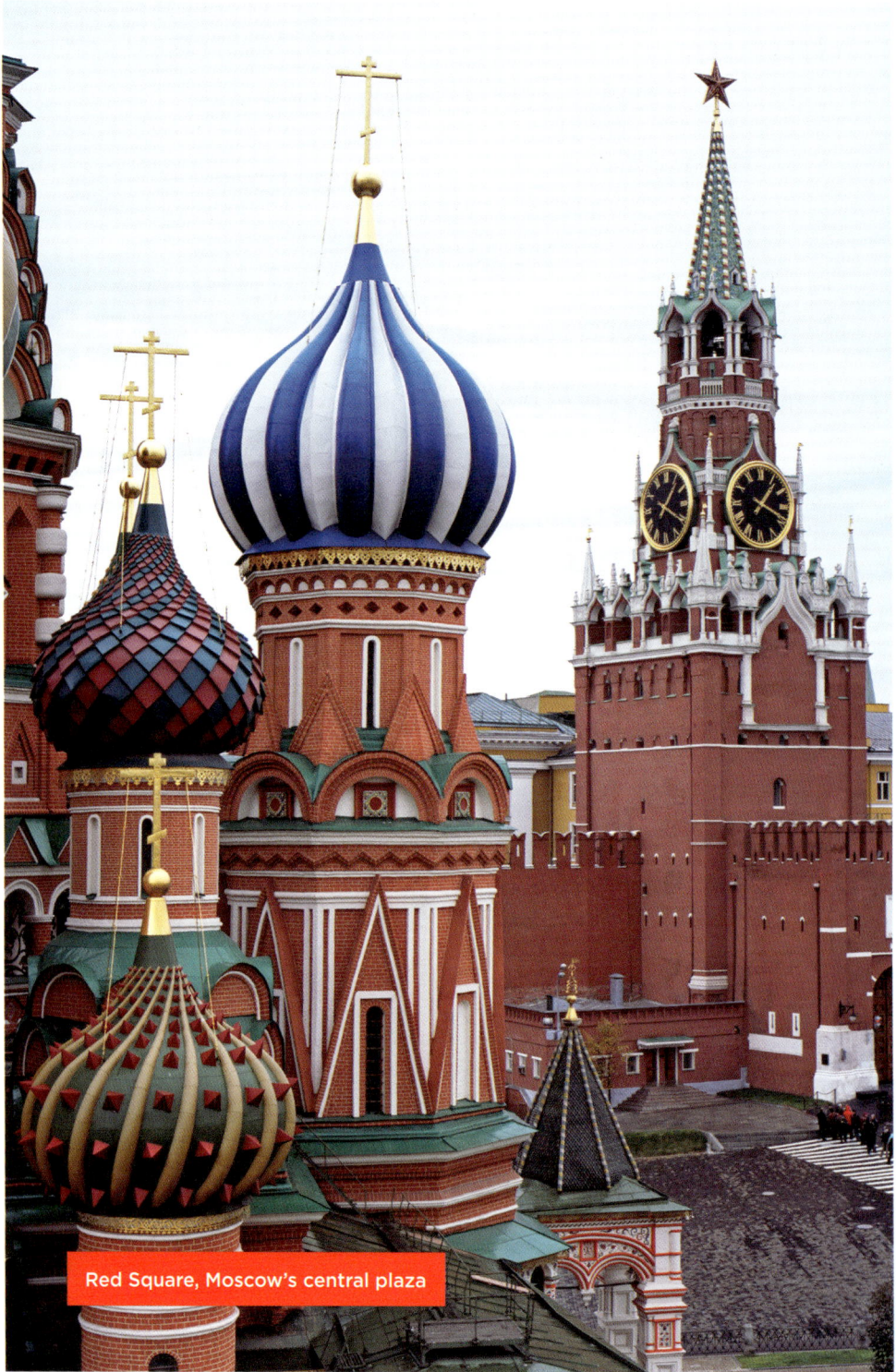
Red Square, Moscow's central plaza

CONTENTS

Introduction

In 1565, the ruthless Russian leader Ivan the Terrible created a 6,000-member security force called the Oprichnina. Officers of this force dressed all in black and rode black horses. Tasked with protecting the government, they terrified and terrorized the Russian people, killing thousands whom they blamed for made-up acts of **treason.**

OPPOSITE: Ivan the Terrible [*center, seated*] ruled by fear and demanded absolute loyalty from his people.

Many rulers after Ivan also created their own security forces to spy on Russian citizens at home or living outside the country. Russian spy agencies instilled an intense amount of fear in people. They were well known for using cruel tactics on their opponents inside and outside Russia—from sending dissidents to forced hospital "treatments" or concentration camps to using torture and execution.

Exposing secrets is a spy's job, and the agents of Russian spy agencies of the 20th and 21st centuries are some of the world's best. Known at different times as the Cheka, NKVD, KGB, SVR, and FSB, these agencies have added to a long tradition of fear and secrecy to keep the nation secure and ensure that those in power stay in power.

COMPLETE NEWS · The Sun · COMPLETE NEWS

TRUMAN SAYS RUSSIA SET OFF ATOM BLAST

New York World-Telegram

EXPLOSION TOOK PLACE IN RECENT WEEKS

ATOMIC BLAST IN RUSSIA

Journal American — Tells Cabinet Of Test in Russia

EXTRA! Truman Makes Vital Disclosure

TRUMAN SAYS REDS HAVE EXPLODED ATOM!

Russia was able to create an atomic bomb much quicker than expected due to their successful spy operations in the 1940s.

Agency Origins

From the mid-1550s, Russia had been ruled by a string of kinglike leaders called czars. That changed in 1917, when the Russian Revolution overthrew the monarchy. The revolution was quickly followed by a bloody civil war and the establishment of a new kind of **dictatorship** led by the Bolsheviks, who would later become the **Communist** Party.

OPPOSITE: Armed Russian soldiers marched beneath a "Communism" banner in October 1917.

13

To help maintain control of the new government, leader Vladimir Lenin followed the tradition started by Ivan the Terrible: He set up spy agencies. These agencies had two main purposes—to make sure people inside the country were not plotting against the government and to uncover information on activities in other nations that might threaten Russia.

The first spy organization Lenin established in 1917 was called the Cheka (Extraordinary Commission for Combating Counterrevolution and Sabotage). It was headed by Felix Dzerzhinsky, a remarkable spy and con man. Dzerzhinsky's greatest achievement was setting up a fake organization called "The Trust." His agents persuaded several foreign **intelligence** organizations to invest money in it. Lenin's government used that money for its own purposes. Several Russian leaders who had been **exiled** after the revolution were also persuaded to join the fake organization. So were some anti-communist spies. That's how sly the Cheka agency was. Most of the duped individuals were arrested or killed.

In 1922, Russia was renamed the Union of Soviet Socialist Republics (USSR), or Soviet Union. Following Lenin's death in 1924, Joseph Stalin was in charge. He had a reputation for being cruel and suspicious of everyone around him. Under Stalin, the USSR expanded, taking over many Eastern European countries. Stalin also renamed Cheka, calling it the Unified State Political Administration (OGPU). He also gave it the new mission of getting rid of landowning farmers who did not want to join the communist system. Farms were taken away from families. Those who objected were either exiled to remote places, such as the frigid wilderness of Siberia, or killed.

In the 1930s, the OGPU became part of the People's Commissariat for Internal Affairs (NKVD), and its duties were increased. The NKVD not only handled espionage activities, but it also oversaw the country's police force, border patrols, criminal investigation units, domestic armed forces, and prison system. Using the NKVD, Stalin set up a police state that tried to control what everyone in the country said, did, or thought. NKVD agents weeded out any dissidents, who were then imprisoned or killed. Even

Dictator Joseph Stalin led the Soviet Union from 1924 to 1953.

The Okhrana

After the assassination of Czar Alexander II in 1881, his successor, Alexander III, took steps to crack down on possible rebels. Following a long Russian tradition, the czar established a secret police force and intelligence organization he called the Okhrana to keep track of any enemies to the crown. One of the Okhrana's main techniques involved placing agents undercover inside groups of dissidents. The agents not only kept track of what the rebels were planning, but they also often pushed them into carrying out illegal acts. Most often, the dissidents were quickly arrested and exiled to Siberia.

Members of the Okhrana

many of the men who had joined Lenin and Stalin in the Russian Revolution were rounded up and executed. Stalin terrorized the people under his rule until his death in 1953.

At the onset of World War II (1939–45), the NKVD expanded Soviet spying activities into other countries, particularly the United States and Great Britain. Soviet leaders were worried that capitalist countries (which believed in free trade and private ownership of property) would try to undermine their communist system of government. A major effort was undertaken to convince U.S. and British citizens, including intelligence officers of both countries, to spy for the Soviet Union. In fact, several high-ranking intelligence officers did become **double agents**. They provided the Soviet Union with key information about British and U.S. espionage activities and revealed the identities of many **operatives** spying inside the USSR.

The **recruiting** effort in the United States accelerated once the country began developing atomic bombs in the mid-1940s. Soviet leaders felt their country must also have nuclear weapons. The push to uncover nuclear secrets was the start of a 46-year competition between the United States and the Soviet Union that became known as the **Cold War** (1945–91).

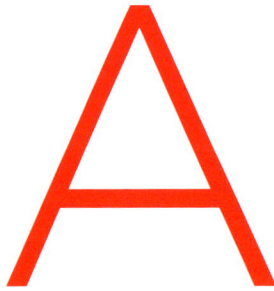

After Stalin died in 1953, Georgy Malenkov took control and oversaw the 1954 creation of a new spy agency, the Committee for State Security (KGB).

The KGB was even more intent than the NKVD had been on controlling everything that went on inside the country. At one time, the KGB was believed to employ as many as 700,000 people both inside and outside the Soviet Union. Everyone living in the USSR or visiting the country came under the KGB's careful watch.

The KGB was organized into a series of 17 divisions called directorates. The First Chief Directorate handled foreign intelligence and placed agents in countries throughout the world. (Intelligence agencies in foreign countries assumed that nearly all Soviet embassy personnel stationed abroad spent at least part of their time spying for the KGB.) The Second Chief Directorate oversaw counterintelligence operations inside the Soviet Union the same way that the Federal Bureau of Investigation (FBI) does in the United States. Other directorates were

Mikhail Gorbachev was the last Soviet leader, serving until the dissolution of the USSR in 1991.

responsible for anti-terrorism, military security, internal security, and the monitoring of foreign communications.

The KGB itself came to an end in 1991 when officers of the organization tried to overthrow Russian leader Mikhail Gorbachev. The effort failed, and Gorbachev ordered the KGB to close. The Soviet Union, too, fell apart at this time. In 1992, parts of the old KGB were put into place in the Ministry of Security and then renamed the Federal Counterintelligence Service (FSK). This intelligence agency was under the president's control. A few years later, Russian president Boris Yeltsin gave the agency yet another name, the Federal Security Service (FSB). He also gave it more power, allowing FSB agents to do intelligence work inside Russia and abroad and enter private homes. Today, the FSB has very little oversight and a lot of power.

Fact vs. Fiction

The KGB (and its successor, the FSB) is the organization that is portrayed in most movies or television shows that feature Russian spies. In 1963, James Bond battled spies in the movie *From Russia with Love*. From 2013 to 2018, *The Americans* TV show told the story of Soviet **sleeper spies** in the United States during the Cold War. Author Tom Clancy's Jack Ryan character has worked with and against Russian spies in more than 30 books, several movies, and a TV series.

OPPOSITE: Daniela Bianchi and Sean Connery star in the espionage thriller *From Russia with Love.*

These fictional spies had thick, Russian accents. They led action-packed, thrilling lives, risking everything for their country in often super-human ways.

For real-life KGB spies, however, life was likely much different. Most of them looked and dressed like average people. They took language classes to lose any trace of an accent. They tried to blend in wherever they went. The same goal of blending in remains true for FSB agents today. Only a small percentage of them do undercover spy work as seen in movies, such as eavesdropping on conversations, breaking into safes to steal secret documents, or taking on enemy agents in hand-to-hand combat. For most agents, their main job is to recruit **assets**. These sources can be average citizens, scientists, or intelligence officers in the countries in which they served. They are groomed by their FSB handler to gather information.

The best spies are those that blend in easily with a crowd of people.

The handler then relays the information to agency officers and pays the asset.

Spies working for the FSB fall into two categories: legals and illegals. Legals work under their own names in a foreign country, usually for the Russian embassy or for a Russian news agency. If they are caught spying, they are usually arrested and deported. Illegals, on the other hand, use made-up names and identities and often work undercover. If caught spying, they could be imprisoned for a long time or even executed. Two types of illegals often used by the FSB are moles and sleepers.

Moles work underground, or in hiding, often with an enemy's intelligence service or in a top-secret laboratory or military base. They sneak out confidential data and turn it over during secret meetings with their handlers. A sleeper is someone with a Russian connection who is given a new identity in a foreign country. Sleepers live ordinary lives in their new country but might be asked to spy under certain circumstances.

The life of an FSB operative can be stressful and dangerous. Operatives are constantly at risk of being discovered and prosecuted. They sense additional pressure from their supervisors. Just as Russian citizens and foreigners visiting the Soviet Union were watched closely by KGB agents, today's FSB spies based in foreign countries are always under observation by their agency to make sure they do not defect or become double agents.

Given the pressures of being part of the FSB, why would anyone willingly choose to participate? One answer is perks. The Russian government extends incentives for doing risky work. In general, FSB agents and their families live better lives, in nicer homes, and receive higher wages than average Russian citizens. They are also given high military ranks that improve their social status. Recruits are especially attracted to the FSB's First Chief Directorate, the foreign intelligence corps. Members of this directorate can live in a foreign country and enjoy luxuries not often available in Russia.

The FSB looks for certain types of people to become First Chief Directorate operatives. Most of them are graduates of respected colleges and universities in Russia. Applicants with science and engineering degrees

The FSB Alpha Group, which specializes in anti-terrorism

are especially desirable. Recruits are also expected to speak one or more foreign languages fluently. They are put through a two-year training program located near Moscow. Classes include the use of ciphers (codes), training in martial arts, and lessons in how to use explosives or other methods for damaging military and technical equipment—skills collectively called tradecraft. Recruits also take courses in communist history and economics. They receive additional training in foreign languages, laws, and customs to help them keep their cover while on assignment.

The story of Gennadi Varenik, from the 1980s, demonstrates some of the problems and temptations Russian agents face in foreign countries. Varenik, a KGB major whose father had also worked for the KGB, was stationed in Bonn, Germany. He spent a year in the offices of the

Soviet news agency TASS to build his cover as a journalist. In Germany, he was introduced to an American spy from the Central Intelligence Agency (CIA). Each man tried, unsuccessfully, to recruit the other as a double agent. Then, a few years later, Varenik found himself in trouble. Tempted by the good life in Germany, Varenik had overspent his KGB salary. He had used funds from his office budget for personal expenses and was afraid of being found out. He was also concerned that one of the local spies he had recruited was really a German agent. He was worried the agent had been providing Varenik with disinformation, which he had relayed to Moscow.

In March 1985, Varenik contacted his CIA "friend" and agreed to spy for the United States. For $3,000 a month, he provided important information about the work of KGB operatives in Germany. Whenever

Varenik wanted to meet his CIA contact, he would make a chalk mark on a telephone pole near the TASS office. This process went on for seven months. Then, Varenik received a message telling him to return with his family to Moscow to discuss a new assignment. He didn't have time to alert the CIA before he was hustled back to the Soviet Union. When no chalk marks showed up in Bonn for several weeks, the Americans suspected that there was a problem. It turned out that Varenik's identity as a double agent had been revealed by a CIA officer working as a double agent. When Varenik returned to Moscow, he was arrested, tried for treason, and executed.

Scare Tactic

In 1957, when the USSR launched Sputnik, the first manufactured satellite, its plan was to experiment with a new way of spying on other countries. An underlying purpose of the launch was to intimidate Americans. While viewing film footage of the large rocket that propelled the small satellite into space, many Americans became convinced that a nuclear attack might soon be launched. Couldn't such a rocket carry nuclear weapons to the United States, they reasoned? Although that would not have been possible, Soviet leader Nikita Khrushchev left the possibility open. "We simply switch the warhead," he boasted.

Gadgets Galore

Part of the fun and excitement
of a spy movie is seeing all the
high-tech vehicles, gadgets,
and weapons the agents use.
But are the high-speed cars
equipped with lasers and the mini
submarines used for underwater
escapes realistic? How about
the microscopic devices that
spies plant to eavesdrop on
conversations or the miniaturized
cameras they use to photograph
documents or secret meetings?

Some of the high-tech devices are the products of filmmakers' imaginations. However, intelligence agencies such as the FSB do spend a lot of time and money developing gadgets and weapons for their agents to use. The goal is always smaller, lighter, faster, and quieter. And if a device winds up looking just like a common, everyday item, so much the better.

In the days of the KGB, in the late 1970s, one devious device was an umbrella used to kill a Bulgarian anticommunist leader named Georgi Markov in London. KGB engineers converted the tip of the umbrella into a silenced gun that could fire a poison pellet. A Soviet agent "accidentally" brushed against Markov on a London bridge, fired the pellet into his leg, and then apologized for bumping into him. Markov died mysteriously four days later.

KGB technicians created plenty of unusual and deadly weapons. One was a cigarette pack adapted to hide a canister of acid. An agent could press a firing device on the outside of the pack to send an acidic spray into a victim's face. By the time the victim fell to the ground, the agent could have easily fled the scene. Another device was a cylinder-shaped gun that could be concealed inside a rolled-up newspaper. Different models of such guns could fire bullets or spray poison gas. KGB agents using the gas gun were supplied with an antidote to the poison just in case they accidentally breathed in the gas themselves. Such an antidote was also needed by KGB agents who used a poison-gas firing device hidden in a specially designed wallet. The wallet had an opening out of which the gas could be propelled and a pocket for storing the antidote tablets.

Not all KGB gadgets were designed to kill. Some were created for eavesdropping and photographing. Others were made for hiding and transferring information. One special spy camera could be strapped around an agent's body to take pictures through an opening in a tiepin. Another camera was hidden inside a hollowed-out compartment of a book, its lens pointing through an opening. To take pictures, the spy would press on the book cover and activate a shutter button. Tiny cameras were also sometimes concealed inside briefcases, cigarette packs, wristwatches, and coat buttons.

KGB technicians developed several **bugs** for recording conversations. One of the most famous bugs was planted inside the U.S. Embassy in Moscow. In 1946, a group of Russian children presented a 2-foot-round (0.6-meter) replica of the Great Seal of the United States to U.S. ambassador Averell Harriman as a gift. Harriman hung it on the wall behind his desk in Moscow. He never suspected that a special transmitter was hidden inside the seal behind the symbol of a bald eagle. The transmitter was activated by an outside radio signal. The bug wasn't discovered until 1952, when the U.S. National Security Agency (NSA) was sweeping the embassy, looking for listening devices. The bug was removed, but its discovery was not made public for several years. Then, in 1960, the United States displayed the device before the United Nations (UN) Security Council to demonstrate unethical behavior on the part of the USSR.

One problem that members of all intelligence agencies have is how to best conceal and transfer documents. In the past, agents had to hide rolls of film, microphotographs, and documents—physical items. Things weren't digital like they are now. KGB technicians once created some clever hiding devices that resembled household products, such as a hollowed-out shaving cream can. Today, FSB agents can use smartphones, surveillance devices, and data monitoring. With a click or a swipe, they can instantly send information and pictures of documents back to Russia.

While gadgets such as hollow coins or tiepin cameras were needed for spying on the ground, KGB aircraft experts designed different types of satellites, airplanes, and balloons for spying from the sky. In October 1957, the Soviet Union stunned people around the world when it launched Sputnik. Such artificial satellites opened new avenues to spies. Now a country's intelligence service could photograph large areas of a foreign country without being detected and then analyze the film for

Crossing the Bridge

The United States and the USSR spent a lot of effort searching for and prosecuting spies during the Cold War. If caught, these spies were often given harsh prison sentences. Later, they might be set free in exchange for the release of a spy from the opposing side. In 1962, for example, Soviet spy Rudolf Abel was swapped for a U.S. pilot named Francis Gary Powers, who had flown a spy plane illegally over Soviet airspace two years earlier. During the swap, the men passed each other on the Glienicke Bridge between East and West Berlin. That bridge was the site of several other important spy swaps.

information about military activity. Satellites could also intercept radio communications. As the value of having satellites increased, so did the need to recruit technical and communications experts who could work with the information satellites collected.

Technology has changed how the FSB agency works. All agents must have solid computer skills. In 1995, an intelligence agent needed to read 20,000 words a day to stay up to date on a low-priority country. In 2016, that amount had risen to 200,000 words a day. Today's

artificial intelligence (AI) has the ability to quickly comb through large amounts of information and highlight key points, summarize, and problem solve, allowing for much more efficient use of an agent's time. The Internet and social media make it easy to track people of interest and

"THE INTERNET AND SOCIAL MEDIA MAKE IT EASY TO TRACK PEOPLE OF INTEREST AND GAIN VALUABLE INSIGHT."

gain valuable insight. Smartphones can be hacked or used as audio/video transmitters. Uncrewed aircraft called drones can be used to collect images and videos, deliver documents, and damage or destroy targets. Drones are controlled by agents on the ground, often tucked into secret places, keeping them out of harm's way.

THE FSB

Notable Agents

From the 1920s until the KGB was disbanded in 1991, the directors of Russian spy agencies were powerful, cruel individuals. And today's FSB is built upon their work. Felix Dzerzhinsky formed the Trust to trap anti-communists and ruthlessly eliminated people he thought might threaten the new communist government. His successor, Vyacheslav Menzhinsky, oversaw the killing of millions of Ukrainian farmers.

OPPOSITE: For his impenetrable commitment to strengthening Soviet intelligence, Felix Dzerzhinsky earned the nickname "Iron Felix."

Menzhinsky was followed by Genrikh Yagoda, who was an expert on poisons and torture. Yagoda was in charge when Stalin ordered the deaths of thousands of communist leaders whom he feared might become powerful enough to rise up against him. Yagoda came under the same suspicion and was so good at his job that Stalin decided to have him killed as well.

Perhaps the most influential Russian spymaster of all was Lavrenti Beria, who ran the NKVD during and after World War II. It was Beria who sent Soviet agents to penetrate intelligence agencies and scientific labs in the United States and Great Britain from the 1930s to the 1950s. Beria's spies recruited moles in both countries, including several high-ranking leaders of Britain's MI5 (domestic intelligence) and MI6 (foreign intelligence) divisions. They also gathered secrets from both countries that helped the Soviet Union build its first nuclear weapons.

Lee Harvey Oswald

In 1959, Lee Harvey Oswald defected from the United States and denounced his U.S. citizenship. The KGB, learning this news, decided to bug his apartment in Minsk. They were considering whether to recruit him as a spy for the KGB. They quickly learned, however, that Oswald couldn't shoot straight, was extremely uncoordinated, and "couldn't figure out how to put film in a simple Russian camera." The KGB claimed it never recruited him (due to his lack of skills). In 1963, Oswald went on to assassinate U.S. president John F. Kennedy.

After Stalin died in 1953, Beria believed he would succeed him as leader of the country. Unfortunately for Beria, his rivals had him quickly eliminated. No one is sure what happened to Beria. Some people suspect that a rumor about the CIA— claiming that Beria was one of its assets in the USSR—may have led to the spy's death.

While the country's spymasters were known for their outright ruthlessness, Russia's most successful spies were notable for being sneaky and clever. One Soviet spy who provided valuable information to Moscow during the early days of World War II was Leopold Trepper. Trepper was a Polish communist who was brought to Moscow in the mid-1930s for special training. He was then sent to Belgium to set up a spy network that would track the German army's movements. Trepper created a fake clothing firm called the Foreign Excellent Raincoat

Company to disguise the work of his spy group. When Germany invaded France in 1940, Trepper moved to Paris and contracted with the Germans to provide raincoats for their soldiers. The arrangement allowed the Soviet spies to meet with German officers and learn a lot about their plans. Trepper quickly had more than 200 spies working for him.

Trepper discovered that Germany planned to invade the Soviet Union, even though the two countries were supposed to be allies. At first, Stalin refused to believe the information, but Trepper kept sending more details that finally convinced him. Because Trepper's spy group sent so many radio transmissions to Moscow, the Germans began calling them the "Red Orchestra." The Germans later captured most of the orchestra members, including Trepper. He avoided execution by agreeing to

Melita Norwood

In 1999, a British woman named Melita Norwood held a press conference to announce she had worked as a Russian spy for 40 years. She was 87 years old. She had been a member of the Communist Party in England and wanted to help spread communism to the West. She would sneak into her boss's office, open the safe, and take pictures of secret documents. She relayed information about nuclear weapons projects and other secret files. She even visited Moscow and was given an award for her service in 1979. Nobody ever knew!

act as a double agent. However, he worded the messages he sent to Moscow in such a way that the Soviets knew they were false. Trepper later escaped and lived out the war in hiding.

After World War II ended and the Cold War began, Soviet intelligence agencies focused their efforts on penetrating Western countries such as West Germany, Great Britain, and the United States. One man recruited to spy in Germany was a British intelligence officer named George Blake. This double agent revealed a number of key secrets. For example, in 1953, he let the Soviets know about a secret tunnel the Americans had built in Berlin for the purpose of tapping phones in Russian and East German offices. The Soviets didn't let on that they knew about the tunnel for three years. In the meantime, they began providing false information on their phones and hoped the Americans were listening. In 1956, the Soviets "accidentally" discovered the tunnel, which was quickly closed down.

The Soviets also set up their own spy networks in the United States and Great Britain. The U.S. network was run by KGB colonel Rudolf Abel. One of the men Abel trained was Gordon Lonsdale, whom the Soviets then sent to London to establish his own spy ring. Lonsdale's group helped the Soviets discover confidential information about the work of the recently established North Atlantic Treaty Organization (NATO). NATO is a military alliance of Western countries focused on checking the expansion of communist influence and furthering democracy in Europe.

Robert Hanssen

Later in the Cold War, the Soviets managed to recruit several moles inside the FBI and CIA. Two of the most famous agents were Robert Hanssen and Aldrich Ames. For more than 20 years, Hanssen, whose FBI job was to catch spies, worked undercover for the KGB and SVR. He left dozens of packages containing U.S. intelligence data at drop sites in the Washington, D.C., area. In return, Hanssen was paid more than $600,000 in cash and diamonds—but he ended up serving a lifetime sentence in U.S. federal prison, dying in 2023. Ames worked as a case officer for the CIA for more than 30 years. Starting in 1985, he began selling secrets to the Soviets, receiving payments of more than $2 million. Some of the information Ames provided included names of undercover agents working for the United States and Great Britain inside Russia. Many of these operatives ended up in Russian prisons or were killed. Ames's spying was finally uncovered in 1994. His arrest sent shock waves through the CIA, and he received life imprisonment.

Another interesting KGB agent was Vladimir Putin. Putin worked for the KGB for 15 years before becoming a politician. He recruited East Germans to steal intelligence and technology from Western countries. After an unremarkable career in the KGB, he quickly rose to power and was named director of the FSB in 1998 by

President Yeltsin. He ultimately became the president of Russia. In that role, Putin overhauled the FSB to continue to give it more power at his disposal. Under Putin, the FSB tamps down protest movements inside Russia. It keeps tabs on all U.S. citizens and other foreign nationals inside its borders. It also arrests U.S. reporters and athletes at will, charges them with espionage, and holds them in prison. "Today, the FSB is incredibly powerful and unaccountable," said Boris Bondarev, a Russian diplomat who resigned and went into hiding in 2022. "Anyone can designate someone else as a foreign spy to get promoted. If you are an FSB officer and you want a quick promotion, you find some spies."

On a Mission

Most spy missions are designed to obtain inside information—secrets that others want to keep hidden. Sometimes the best way to do that is to find an insider and convert them.

OPPOSITE: Stealing atomic bomb-making secrets was a top priority for Soviet spies and their assets in the 1940s.

One important Russian mission involved getting inside Great Britain's main intelligence agencies, MI5 and MI6. The Soviets accomplished this by recruiting five graduates of England's prestigious Cambridge University and encouraging them to join the British government or intelligence services. The "Cambridge Five"—Kim Philby, Guy Burgess, Donald Maclean, Anthony Blunt, and John Cairncross—all belonged to communist organizations in college. They agreed to spy for the Russians largely because of their pro-communist belief.

As they rose in the government ranks in the 1940s, two of the Cambridge Five, Philby and Maclean, were given assignments in the United States. There they learned many secrets about the development of the atomic bomb and passed them along to the Soviets. Philby also had access to reports of U.S. efforts to discover which atomic

scientists might be revealing secrets of their work to the Russians. He warned the KGB about these reports so that they could protect their assets from being discovered.

Philby was able to keep his spying so secret that he earned promotion after promotion in MI6 and was in line to become the organization's head in 1951. Then Maclean and Burgess came under investigation for spying and defected to the Soviet Union. Philby was watched carefully after that and decided to join his colleagues in Russia in the early 1960s when it became clear that he, too, might be arrested. He was later given the rank of general in the KGB. Blunt and Cairncross remained in England.

The atomic bomb was the focus of another important Russian spy mission in the 1940s. The Soviets were determined to build their own bomb but decided to take a shortcut by stealing secrets from nuclear scientists working on the bomb in the United States. One scientist more than willing to reveal what he knew was Klaus Fuchs. Fuchs had escaped from Germany before World War II and become a British citizen. Then he came to the the United States to work on the atomic bomb research team called the Manhattan Project. Like the Cambridge Five, Fuchs was a communist, so he was easy for the KGB to recruit. Fuchs was living in the United States and conveyed atomic research secrets to the Russians. After the war, Fuchs's spying was discovered, and he was arrested and imprisoned in England.

Julius Rosenberg and his wife, Ethel, were Russian agents living in New York. They provided atomic bomb details to a Soviet handler. Ethel's brother worked on the Manhattan Project and would relay information to her. After the Soviets tested their own bomb in 1949, the FBI intensified its efforts to find possible Manhattan Project leaks. The Rosenbergs were discovered, arrested, and later executed for conspiracy to commit espionage.

During the Cold War, both the Soviets and the Americans concentrated on sneaking into each other's intelligence services. They spent almost as much time trying to discover which of their own intelligence officers might be double agents. One agent who ended up on both sides was Dmitri Polyakov. In 1951, Polyakov was sent to New York as part of the Soviet delegation to the UN. His real purpose was to spy on the United States, which he did successfully for five years. He returned to the USSR in 1956. He became very angry when Russian officials would not let him bring his son to New York for an important medical operation. After the boy died, it is thought that Polyakov blamed his bosses and decided

Dmitri Polyakov

to change sides. When the KGB sent Polyakov back to the United States in 1961, he offered his services to the CIA. In his double-agent role, Polyakov began sending disinformation to Russia about new chemical weapons the Americans were developing. The CIA hoped the Russians would waste a lot of time and money trying to copy these useless plans. Polyakov worked as a double agent for more than 20 years until he was exposed by both Robert Hanssen and Aldrich Ames in the 1980s and later executed in Russia.

Sometimes the FSB is the agency tasked with dealing with terrorists. In 2002, a rebel group invaded a theater in Moscow. It took hundreds of people hostage. FSB units were able to help rescue many of them, but after two days, FSB forces filled the entire theater with a powerful gas. The gas was meant to disable the rebels, but instead, it killed more than 150 people, including the terrorists. Two years later, a school was taken hostage by terrorists. Again, the FSB was called to handle the situation. The FSB helped attack and eliminate the terrorist group but was criticized for the large number of casualties. More than 330 people, mostly children, lost their lives. The

FSB then went on a mission to hunt down the terrorist leader responsible for the school tragedy. Two years later, in 2006, it was successful in assassinating him.

Since the KGB disbanded in 1991, espionage has changed. While most spy missions of the NKVD and KGB focused on military secrets, the work of the FSB has a wider reach. Many of its missions aim to learn about new products being made by companies around the world. FSB agents have tried to sneak into technology laboratories and businesses in countries such as Germany, Israel, China, and South Korea, as well as the United States, to learn about new types of computers, aircraft, vehicles, and robots. FSB computer experts have also hacked into the systems of important technology companies to learn more secrets. In 2024 the FBI and their allies disrupted a Russian network of more than 1,000 hacked Internet routers. The FSB was using the routers for espionage operations against foreign governments, gathering military, security, and corporate secrets. The FBI called this tactic a botnet.

Why are FSB agents focusing on industrial espionage? The Russian government and business leaders believe Russian companies can save a lot of money developing new products if they have inside information. One German expert estimates that Russian spies steal up to $5 billion in industrial secrets from Germany each year and billions more from other countries. Meanwhile, the FSB has increased its counterespionage efforts to make sure that Russian technology secrets are not likewise revealed to other countries.

In 2022, Russia invaded Ukraine. The FSB's power is so vast that some experts believe the invasion was

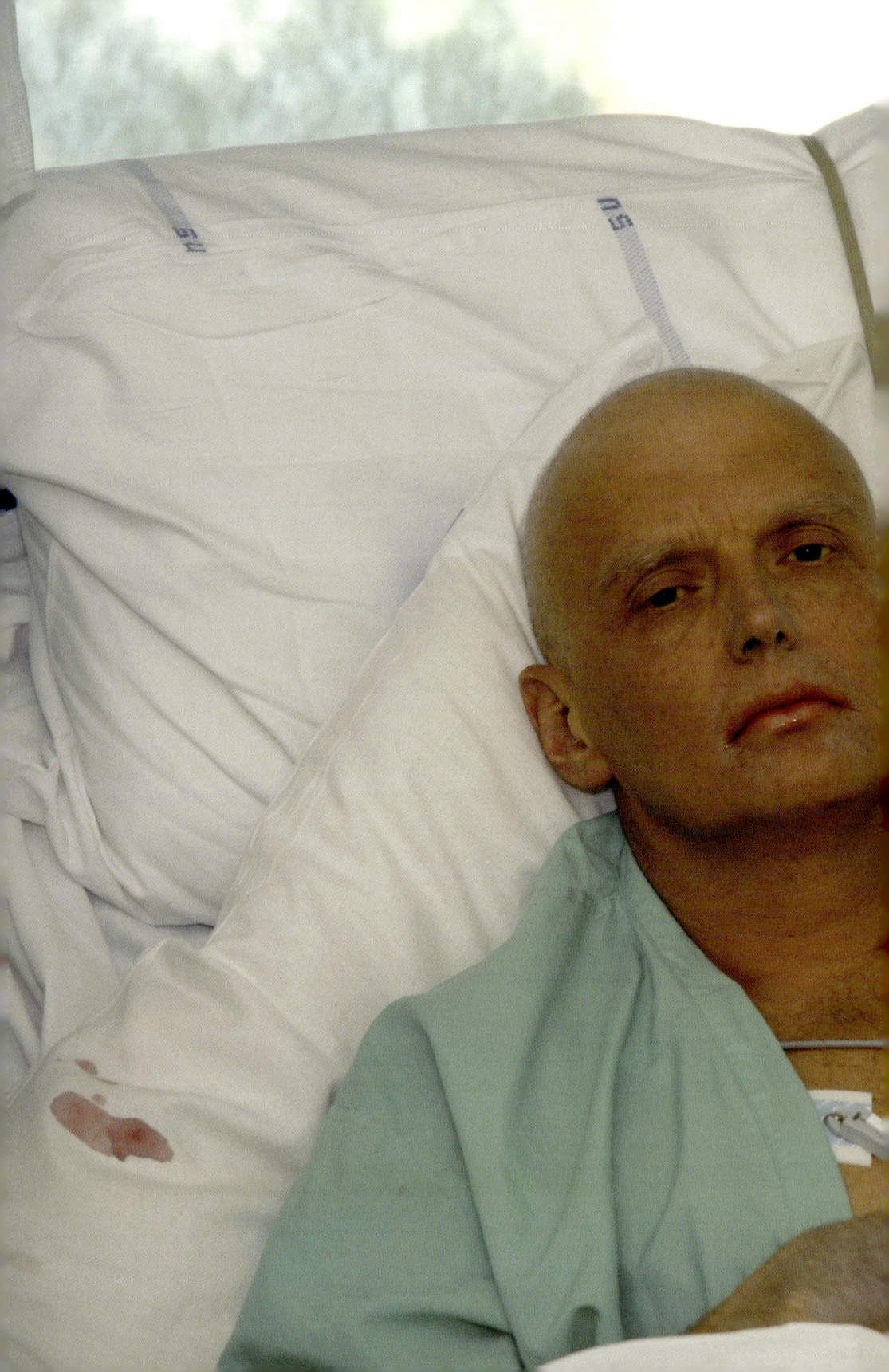

Don't Drink the Tea

Alexander Litvinenko was a KGB and FSB agent who accused his superiors of corruption in 1998. They immediately sentenced him to nine years in prison, but Litvinenko fled to London with his family and began working for British Intelligence. In 2006, while investigating the assassination of a Russian journalist, Litvinenko mysteriously died of radiation poisoning. An investigation found that his tea had been laced with a chemical element called polonium during a meeting with two Russian agents. Investigators supposed that the agents were sent by the FSB to kill him. The European Court of Human Rights reached the same conclusion in 2021.

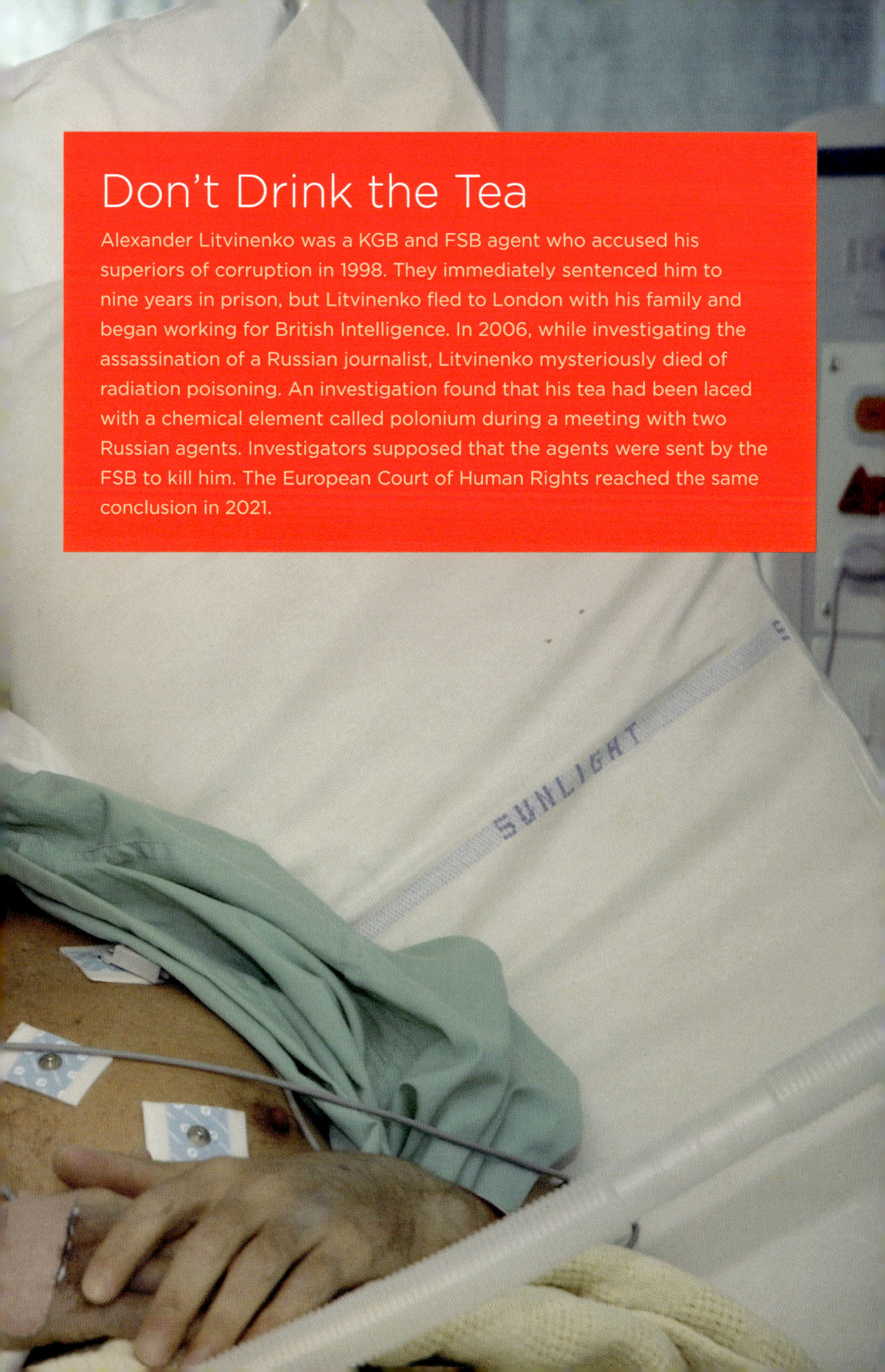

Russian president Vladimir Putin

planned entirely by the agency. FSB intelligence had assured President Putin that Russia could quickly overtake Ukraine. But the intelligence proved wrong. As of July 2024, the conflict was still going.

Putin has repeatedly told Russian citizens that the FSB is a very different organization from earlier Russian intelligence agencies. The old agencies, he said, were designed to repress Russians' human rights, while the new one is charged with defending democracy in Russia. Human rights activists, however, disagree. They believe the Russian spy agency is up to its old tricks. In 2020, the FSB botched a poisoning of Alexei Navalny, a vocal activist opposed to Putin. Navalny eventually died four years later under suspicious circumstances in a Russian prison. FSB doctors claim it was a blood clot. Navalny's family claims the FSB poisoned him. It's likely no one will ever know for sure.

Are the days of terror tactics by the Russian secret police over? Are dissidents in Russia no longer under threat of being exiled to Siberia? Will the FSB ever free itself of its ruthless roots going back to Ivan the Terrible? It's difficult to say. The FSB is a highly skilled intelligence organization, one of the best in the world, and it does an expert job of keeping its work hidden from the eyes of outsiders. Russia, the world's largest country in terms of total area, remains one of the most unknown. And as long as there are secrets to uncover, there will be spies tasked with that mission.

A mass grave discovered outside a former NKVD prison in Ukraine holds many secrets.

Selected Bibliography

Andrew, Christopher, and Oleg Gordievsky. *KGB: The Inside Story of Its Foreign Operations from Lenin to Gorbachev.* New York: HarperCollins, 1990.

Crowdy, Terry. *The Enemy Within: A History of Espionage.* Oxford; New York: Osprey, 2006.

The Dossier Center. "Lubyanka Federation: How the FSB Determines the Politics and Economics of Russia." The Atlantic Council. October 5, 2020. https://www.atlanticcouncil.org/in-depth-research-reports/report/lubyanka-federation.

Hershkovitz, Shay. "How Tech Is Transforming the Intelligence Industry." TechCrunch. August 10, 2019. https://techcrunch.com/2019/08/10/how-tech-is-transforming-the-intelligence-industry.

Mahl, Tom E. *Espionage's Most Wanted: The Top 10 Book of Malicious Moles, Blown Covers, and Intelligence Oddities.* Washington, D.C.: Brassey's, 2003.

Parkinson, Joe, and Drew Hinshaw. "Inside the Secretive Russian Security Force That Targets Americans." *The Wall Street Journal.* July 7, 2023. https://www.wsj.com/articles/fsb-evan-gershkovich-russia-security-force-dkro-e9cf9a49.

Soldatov, Andrei. "Putin Has Finally Reincarnated the KGB." *Foreign Policy Magazine.* September 21, 2016. https://foreignpolicy.com/2016/09/21/putin-has-finally-reincarnated-the-kgb-mgb-fsb-russia.

Volkman, Ernest. *Spies: The Secret Agents Who Changed the Course of History.* New York: J. Wiley, 1994.

Glossary

agent   a person who works for, but is not necessarily officially employed by, an intelligence service

asset   a hidden source acting as a spy or providing secret information to a spy

botnet   a group of Internet-connected computers infected with a virus (malware) used to carry out cyber attacks; the term comes from the words *robot* and *network*

bug   a hidden recording/listening device

Cold War   the hostile competition between the United States and its allies against the Soviet Union and its allies that began at the end of World War II and lasted until the collapse of the Soviet Union in 1991

communist   related to a political and economic system in which all goods and property are owned by the state and shared by all members of the public

counterintelligence

efforts made by a nation's intelligence agency to catch and eliminate spies working against the country and protect the country against sabotage or terrorism; also called counterespionage

defect	to leave a country forever in favor of another
dictatorship	a form of government in which one person or group rules with absolute power, often in an oppressive way
dissident	a person who disagrees with and rebels against a government
double agent	a spy for one country who doubles as a spy for a second country and often provides false information to the first country
espionage	the act of spying
exile	to bar someone from their native country, usually for political reasons
intelligence	information uncovered and transmitted by a spy
mole	an employee of one intelligence service who actually works for another service or who works undercover in a foreign country to supply intelligence
operative	an undercover agent working for an intelligence agency
recruiting	the process of hiring or enlisting
sleeper spy	an operative placed in a target country or organization long before they're asked to actively spy
spy ring	a group or network of spies working together
treason	the crime of betraying one's country

Websites

Federal Security Service
https://www.britannica.com/topic/Federal-Security-Service
Read a brief history of the FSB.

The International Spy Museum
https://www.spymuseum.org
Explore bios of real-life agents and frequently asked questions
about spying.

KGB
https://www.history.com/topics/european-history/kgb
Learn about the Soviet Union's KGB and how it became the
FSB.

Index